CHAPTER 1: INTRODUCTION

Importance of Mental Well-Being

Mental well-being is crucial for leading a fulfilling and balanced life. It affects how we think, feel, and act, influencing our daily interactions, decisions, and overall quality of life. Taking steps to improve our mental health is just as important as maintaining physical health, and this guide aims to provide practical strategies to help you boost your mood and enhance your well-being.

Overview of the Guide

This guide is structured to cover various aspects of well-being, from understanding your emotions to building positive relationships and managing stress. Each chapter provides actionable tips and techniques to help you on your journey to better mental health. Let's embark on this journey together and explore how you can create a more joyful and fulfilling life.

Table of Contents

6. **Stress Management Techniques**
- Identifying Stressors
- Relaxation Techniques
- Time Management Strategies

7. **Developing a Positive Mindset**
- Power of Positive Thinking
- Gratitude Journaling
- Affirmations and Visualization

8. **Engaging in Hobbies and Interests**
- Finding Your Passion
- Benefits of Creative Activities
- Balancing Work and Play

9. **Setting and Achieving Goals**
- SMART Goals Framework
- Overcoming Procrastination
- Celebrating Small Wins

10. **Professional Help and Support**
- When to Seek Professional Help
- Types of Therapy
- Support Groups and Resources

11. **Conclusion**
- Recap of Key Points
- Encouragement for Ongoing Practice

CHAPTER 2: UNDERSTANDING YOUR EMOTIONS

Recognizing Different Emotions

Emotions are complex and multifaceted, ranging from joy and excitement to sadness and anger. Recognizing and naming your emotions is the first step towards understanding and managing them. Keep a daily journal to track your feelings and identify patterns in your emotional responses.

Emotional Triggers

Understanding what triggers certain emotions can help you anticipate and manage them more effectively. Reflect on recent situations that elicited strong emotions and consider the underlying causes. This awareness can empower you to respond more calmly and constructively in the future.

Journaling for Emotional Clarity

Journaling is a powerful tool for gaining insight into your emotions. Set aside time each day to write about your feelings and experiences. This practice can help you process emotions, identify patterns, and develop strategies for handling challenging situations.

CHAPTER 3: HEALTHY LIFESTYLE CHOICES

Nutrition and Mood

What you eat can significantly impact your mood. A balanced diet rich in fruits, vegetables, whole grains, and lean proteins can boost your energy levels and enhance your mental clarity. Avoid excessive sugar and processed foods, which can lead to mood swings and energy crashes.

Exercise and Mental Health

Regular physical activity releases endorphins, which are natural mood lifters. Aim for at least 30 minutes of moderate exercise most days of the week. Activities like walking, swimming, or yoga can reduce stress and improve your overall sense of well-being.

Importance of Sleep

Quality sleep is essential for emotional regulation and mental clarity. Establish a consistent sleep routine, create a restful environment, and avoid stimulants like caffeine before bedtime. Aim for 7-9 hours of sleep each night to feel your best.

CHAPTER 4: MINDFULNESS AND MEDITATION

Basics of Mindfulness

Mindfulness involves paying attention to the present moment without judgment. It helps you become more aware of your thoughts and feelings, reducing stress and enhancing emotional regulation. Practice mindfulness by focusing on your breath, sensations, or surroundings.

Daily Meditation Practices

Meditation is a powerful tool for cultivating mindfulness. Start with short, daily sessions and gradually increase the duration. Guided meditations, breathing exercises, and body scans can help you develop a consistent practice.

Mindfulness in Everyday Activities

Incorporate mindfulness into daily activities such as eating, walking, or washing dishes. By fully engaging in these tasks, you can reduce stress and enhance your overall sense of well-being.

CHAPTER 5: BUILDING POSITIVE RELATIONSHIPS

Social Connections and Happiness

Strong social connections are linked to greater happiness and longevity. Make time to nurture relationships with family, friends, and colleagues. Engage in meaningful conversations and activities that foster a sense of connection and belonging.

Effective Communication Skills

Effective communication is key to building and maintaining healthy relationships. Practice active listening, express your thoughts and feelings clearly, and be open to feedback. Developing these skills can enhance your interactions and reduce misunderstandings.

Setting Healthy Boundaries

Setting boundaries is essential for maintaining your well-being. Communicate your needs and limits clearly and respectfully. Healthy boundaries can prevent burnout, reduce stress, and promote healthier relationships.

CHAPTER 6: STRESS MANAGEMENT TECHNIQUES

Identifying Stressors

Identify the sources of stress in your life, whether they are work-related, personal, or environmental. Understanding what causes your stress can help you develop strategies to manage it more effectively.

Relaxation Techniques

Incorporate relaxation techniques such as deep breathing, progressive muscle relaxation, or guided imagery into your daily routine. These practices can help you reduce stress and promote a sense of calm.

Time Management Strategies

Effective time management can reduce stress and increase productivity. Prioritize tasks, set realistic goals, and break projects into manageable steps. Use tools like planners or digital apps to stay organized and focused.

CHAPTER 7: DEVELOPING A POSITIVE MINDSET

Power of Positive Thinking

Cultivating a positive mindset can significantly impact your mood and overall well-being. Challenge negative thoughts, focus on positive aspects of situations, and practice gratitude. A positive outlook can enhance your resilience and happiness.

Gratitude Journaling

Keeping a gratitude journal involves writing down things you are thankful for each day. This practice can shift your focus from what's wrong to what's right, improving your mood and fostering a sense of contentment.

Affirmations and Visualization

Positive affirmations and visualization techniques can help you reframe negative thoughts and achieve your goals. Repeat affirmations that resonate with you and visualize yourself succeeding in your endeavors.

CHAPTER 8: ENGAGING IN HOBBIES AND INTERESTS

Finding Your Passion

Engaging in activities you are passionate about can boost your mood and provide a sense of fulfillment. Explore different hobbies and interests until you find something that excites and motivates you.

Benefits of Creative Activities

Creative activities like painting, writing, or playing music can be therapeutic and stress-relieving. These activities allow you to express yourself and can be a source of joy and relaxation.

Balancing Work and Play

Striking a balance between work and leisure is essential for your well-being. Schedule time for activities you enjoy and ensure you take breaks to recharge. This balance can prevent burnout and enhance your overall happiness.

CHAPTER 9: SETTING AND ACHIEVING GOALS

SMART Goals Framework

Setting SMART (Specific, Measurable, Achievable, Relevant, Time-bound) goals can help you achieve your aspirations effectively. Break your goals into smaller, manageable steps and track your progress regularly.

Overcoming Procrastination

Procrastination can hinder your progress and increase stress. Identify the reasons behind your procrastination and develop strategies to overcome it, such as breaking tasks into smaller steps and using a timer to stay focused.

Celebrating Small Wins

Acknowledge and celebrate your achievements, no matter how small. Recognizing your progress can boost your motivation and confidence, encouraging you to continue working towards your goals.

CHAPTER 10: PROFESSIONAL HELP AND SUPPORT

When to Seek Professional Help

If you are struggling to manage your emotions or if your mood significantly impacts your daily life, it may be time to seek professional help. Mental health professionals can provide support and guidance tailored to your needs.

Types of Therapy

Various types of therapy, such as cognitive-behavioral therapy (CBT), psychotherapy, or counseling, can help you address mental health challenges. Research different options and find a therapist who suits your needs and preferences.

Support Groups and Resources

Support groups and online communities can provide a sense of connection and understanding. Sharing experiences with others facing similar challenges can be comforting and offer practical advice and support.

CHAPTER 11: CONCLUSION

Recap of Key Points

This guide has covered a range of strategies to help you boost your mood and enhance your well-being. From understanding your emotions and adopting a healthy lifestyle to developing a positive mindset and seeking professional help, each chapter offers practical tips to support your mental health journey.

Encouragement for Ongoing Practice

Improving your well-being is an ongoing process that requires commitment and effort. Continue to practice the techniques and strategies outlined in this guide, and remember that small, consistent steps can lead to significant improvements in your mood and overall quality of life. Stay motivated, stay positive, and take care of yourself.

This comprehensive guide aims to provide you with the tools and knowledge to enhance your mental well-being.

Remember, improving your mood and overall happiness is a journey, and each step you take brings you closer to a more fulfilling and joyful life.

MY NOTES

MY NOTES

MY NOTES

MY NOTES

MY NOTES